HOW TO SPEAK IN PUBLIC

PUBLIC SPEAKING. BUILD SELF-CONFIDENCE, CREATE AN IMPACT ON YOUR AUDIENCE AND MASTER PERSUASION SKILLS

Chery Hammond

CHAPTER NO.1

WHY PUBLIC SPEAKING MATTERS TODAY

WHY IS PUBLIC SPEAKING IMPORTANT?

In today's environment, we are continually swamped with good and bad messages. Regardless of where you live, where you work or go to school, and what type of media you use, you're likely to be exposed to hundreds of people. There are thousands of advertising messages every day. Researcher Norman W. Edmund estimates that the amount of world knowledge will double every 73 days by 2020. Edmond, N.W. (2005). End the most significant educational and intellectual mistake in history: a $ 100,000 challenge for leaders in education. Lauderdale, Fort Florida: Scientific Method Publishing Co. Because we live in a world overwhelmed with content, it is more important than ever to communicate information in a way that is accessible to others. To better understand why public speaking important, you should first consider public speaking in everyday life. Then we discuss how public Speaking can help you personally. Daily Public Speaking Every day, people from the United States and around the world speak and stand in front of a specific audience. In fact, there is also a monthly publication entitled "Vital Speeches of the Day" (http://www.vsotd.com) that captures some of the top speeches in the United States. There are many different types of public Speaking, but they can generally be divided into three categories: informative, compelling, and entertaining based on their intended purpose.

INFORMATIVE SPEAKING

One of the various standard representations of public Speaking is the provision of information. The main purpose of an informative presentation is to share knowledge about the topic with the audience. The reasons for useful speeches are very different. For example, you may be asked to instruct a group of colleagues to use new computer software, or to report to a group of managers on the latest project progress. Local community groups may want to learn about volunteering in New Orleans during the spring vacation. Or you would like your classmates to share their expertise in Mediterranean cuisine. Common to all of these examples is the goal of conveying information to the public. Informational speech is integrated into many different professions. Doctors often teach medical students, other doctors and patients about specialties. Teachers give presentations to both parents and students. Firefighters show how house fires can be effectively combated. Informative Speaking is a common part of many jobs and other daily activities. As a result, learning to speak effectively has become an essential skill in today's world. Convincing Speaking A second common reason to speak to an audience is to convince others. In our daily lives we often convince and motivate others or in other ways to change their beliefs, take action and rethink their decisions. To promote music education in your local school district and encourage customers to buy corporate products or encourage students to college, you need to influence others through public Speaking. For some people, such as for example, elected officials, making convincing speeches is an important part of success and the continuation of professional success. Others make their careers by speaking to groups of people who pay to listen to them. Motivating writers and speakers like Les Brown (http://www.lesbrown.com) make millions of dollars every year from those who want to improve their lives. Another professional speaker and author, Brian Tracy, specializes in helping leaders become more productive and effective at work (http://www.briantracy.com). Whether in public or daily or several times a year, it is not very easy to convince others. Developing effective persuasion skills can be both personal and professional. Entertainment Speaking Entertainment Speaking includes a variety of speeches, from introductions to wedding toasts to awards, award ceremonies, funeral and post-service ceremonies, and after-dinner speeches and motivational speeches. Pleasant Speaking has been outstanding since the days of the ancient Greeks when Aristotle identified contagious Speaking (speaking in a ritual context) as an important way of speaking.

In addition to convincing and informative speeches, from religious leaders to comedians, some experts earn their living by merely giving funny speeches. Speaking to entertain like anyone who has seen an award ceremony on TV or who has seen the most uncoordinated best men make a wedding toast is an adequate preparation, and this is a job that requires practice. According to a comparison by sociologist Andrew Zekeri. Zekeri, AA (2004), the personal benefits of public speaking are the most excellent skills that college graduates find useful in the business world. I did it. The skills and abilities of the college curriculum that former students have determined are essential to their careers. College Student Journal, 38, 412-422. This fact alone is worth learning about public speaking. However, communicating effectively with hundreds of thousands of students taking public courses has many other advantages. Let's take a look at some of the personal benefits that come from both public sessions and public speaking. Benefits of Public Speaking Courses In addition to learning the process of creating and delivering useful language, public speaking students get many other benefits from the class. Some of these advantages are:

- development of critical thinking skills,
- fine-tuning verbal and non-verbal skills,
- Overcome the fear of speaking in public.

Developing critical thinking skills One of the first benefits of speaking publicly is the ability to think critically. Problem-solving is one of the many essential skills of thinking covered in this course. For example, when preparing a convincing speech, you need to consider the real issues that affect campus, community, or the world, and provide possible solutions to those issues. You also need to think about the positive and negative consequences of the solution and share your ideas with others. At first glimpse, it may appear easy to find a solution to campus problems like lack of parking spaces.

Just add more space. However, further research shows that the cost of buildings, the environmental impact of the loss of green space, the need for maintenance or the limited space for additional space make this solution impractical. The ability to think about the problem and analyze the potential costs and benefits of the solution is an integral part of critical thinking and public speaking to convince others. These skills can be useful not only in public but also throughout your life. As previously mentioned, college graduates in Zachary's study found their verbal communication skills to be the most helpful for business success. Public language courses are doubly valuable because the second most important skill they reported was problem-solving! Another benefit of speaking publicly is that you can better conduct and analyze your research. Speakers must provide credible evidence in their speeches when trying to convince different audiences. Therefore, public language courses improve your ability to find and use a variety of sources. Fine-tuning verbal and non-verbal skills Another benefit of courses in public speaking is the ability to fine-tune verbal and non-verbal communication skills. Regardless of whether you have attended public speeches in high school or are speaking to your audience for the first time, you are a comprehensive communicator if you actively practice your communication skills and have the opportunity to get professional feedback. Often people do not even notice that they are spinning their hair and do not speak words repeatedly when speaking in public until they receive feedback from the teacher during the public language course. People in the United States regularly pay more exceeding than $ 100 an hour to language coaches to improve their language skills. Language coaches are built into the classrooms so you can take this opportunity to improve your verbal and non-verbal communication skills. Overcoming Fear of Public Speech Another benefit of taking public speaking courses is that it reduces the fear of public speaking. Most people are concerned when they speak in public, whether they have talked a lot in public or have just started.

THE PROCESS OF PUBLIC SPEAKING

As mentioned earlier, we all come across thousands of messages in our daily environment. Therefore, listening to your ideas more than any other message is a constant struggle. Some speakers try gimmicks, but I firmly believe that listening to a message requires three basic elements: message, skill, and passion. The first part of delivering a message is the message itself. If what you say is clear and consistent, people tend to pay more attention to it. However, if the message is not clear, people often stop paying attention. Our discussion in the first part of this book includes ways to get clear and consistent content. The second part of listening to the message is to develop practical conversation abilities. You may have the most immeasurable faiths in the world, but if you don't have basic speaking skills, you have a problem that no one can hear. This book focuses on the skills you need to effectively share your ideas with others. After all, if you want to hear your message, you have to communicate your passion for it. One mistake that inexperienced speakers make is choosing topics that have no emotional investment. If the audience can say that you really don't care about your topic, they'll just chase you away. Passion is an additional spark that draws people's attention and makes you hear your message. This section examines the process of public speaking by first presenting the basic model of public speaking and then explaining how public speaking works as a dialogue. These models provide a basic understanding of the communication process and some of the challenges you can face as a speaker. Public Speaking Model The basic model of human communication is one of the topics that most communication teachers in each class begin with. To focus on public speaking, we present two models that are often discussed in communication: interactions and transactions.

INTERACTION MODEL

The communication interaction model developed by Wilbur Schramm is based on a linear model. Schram, W. (1954). Communication mechanism. W. Schramm (ed.), Communication Processes and Effects (pp. 3–26). Urbana, Illinois: University of Illinois Press. Schramm added three main components to the Shannon and Weaver models. First, Schramm identified two basic communication processes: coding and decoding. Coding 12 is what the source does when it composes a message, adjusts it to the recipient, and sends it on a channel selected by the source. "Wrench, JS, Makris ken, JC And Richmond, VP (2008) Human Communication in Everyday Life: Explanation and Application Boston, Mass.: Allyn & Bacon, p. 17. While preparing for a speech at home or in front of the classroom if you stand and talk to your colleagues, take part in the encoding process. The second important process is decoding process 13 or "capturing (e.g. listening to or viewing) the source message". Interpret, evaluate the source message and respond to the source message. "" Wrench, JS, McCrisken, JC and Richmond, VP (2008). Human communication in everyday life: description and application. Boston, Mass.: Allyn & Bacon, p. 17. Decoding, When the audience listens to speech, on respects the non-verbal behavior of the speaker and focuses on the presentation devices used by the speaker, this is relevant to the context of public speaking and you have to interpret what you are saying: the int Interpreting the speaker's message may sound simple in theory, but it can actually cause many problems: the speaker's verbal message, non-verbal communication, and mediated presentation support 14 can make the message 15 clearer or less understandable. For example, unfamiliar vocabulary, language that is too fast or too quiet, small printing aids can make it difficult to understand the meaning of the speaker and vice versa the definition of complex terms. Providing gestures, using gestures at the right time and displaying graphs of quantitative information can help speakers help interpret their meaning.

Rate the message after interpreting what the speaker says. Was it good Do you agree with the speaker or not? Is the speaker discussion logical? These are all questions you can ask yourself when evaluating your speech. When the recipient encodes the message and sends it to the source, the final part of the decoding is the "response to the source message". This process is called feedback16 when the recipient sends the message back to the source. Schramm speaks about three types of feedback: through, somewhat personal and complicated. Schram, W. (1954). Connection mechanism. W. Schramm (ed.), Communication Processes and Effects (pp. 3–26). Urbana, Illinois: University of Illinois

Press. The first type, direct feedback, occurs when the receiver interacts directly with the source. For example, if the speech ends with a question and answer period, the listener openly agrees with the speaker or not. The second type of somewhat direct feedback focuses on non-verbal messages that are sent while the caller is speaking. The final type of indirect feedback often has a long-time lag between the actual signal and the recipient's feedback. Suppose you ran for the student president, gave a speech to various groups on campus, and lost on the student's election day. Your audience, the various groups you spoke to, gave indirect feedback on your message through your surveys. One of the challenges for speakers is to respond effectively to audience feedback, unusually direct and moderate direct feedback that is received during a presentation.

TRANSACTIONAL MODEL OF PUBLIC SPEAKING

One of the most significant concerns of some people about the interaction model of communication is the tendency to divide it into the non-overlapping source or recipient categories. With Schramm's model, coding and decoding are perceived differently at the source and at the receiver. Besides, the interaction model cannot handle situations in which multiple sources interact at the same time. Mortenson, C.D. (1972). Communication: A study of human connection. New York, New York: McGraw Hill. To inscribe these vulnerabilities, Dean Barnlund suggested a transaction model for discussion. Burnland, D.C. (2008). The transaction model of interaction. C. D. Mortensen (ed.), Information Theory (2nd ed., pp. 47-57). New Brunswick New Jersey: transaction. The basic requirement of the transaction model is that individuals send and receive messages at the same time. While people are involved in either the source or the recipient role in the interaction model and the meaning of the message is sent from the source to the recipient, the transaction model is that the purpose of both interacting people is correlated. Assume This The idea that the meaning corresponds between people is based on a concept called "field of experience". According to West and Turner, the field of experience includes "how human culture, experience and genetics influence the ability to communicate with others". "West, R. & Turner, LH (2010). Introduction to Communication Theory: Analysis and Application (4th Edition). New York, New York: McGraw-Hill, p. 13. Our Education, Race, Gender, and Ethnicity Religion, personality, beliefs, behaviour, attitudes, language, social status, past experiences and customs are all aspects of the field of expertise that lead to all interactions and require a shared experience that makes it difficult to speak effectively to a viewer who a completely different experience than we have. Our goal as a speaker is to convince the audience is to build on a common area of expertise so that it can help the public. Dialogue theory of public speaking Most people speak publicly, Germany listens passively. We believe that on three of the most general principles is employed in dialogue theory 17:

DIALOGUE VS. MONOLOGUE

The first principle of an interactive perspective is that communication should be a dialogue, not a monologue. Lev Jakbinsky argued that when the audience actively attracted speakers through questions, even situations of public speaking often became dialogues. He even argued that non-verbal behaviour (e.g. nodding and consent) served as feedback to the speaker and even contributed to the dialogue. Yakbinsky, L.P. (1997). Interactive language. (M. Eskin, Trance). PMLA, 112 (2), 249-4. 256. (original work from 1923). Overall, it becomes more aggressive if you look at the experience of speaking publicly as a dialogue.

MEANINGS ARE IN PEOPLE NOT WORDS

The Meaning of Bakhtin, M. (2001a). Problems with the audio genre. (V. W. McGee, Trans., 1986). In P. Bizzell & B. Herzberg (ed.), Rhetorical Traditions (pp. 1227–1245). Boston, MA: Bedford / St. Martin. (Original work, published in 1953.); Bakhtin, M. (2001b). Marxism and philosophy of language. (L. Matejka& amp; I.R. Titunik, Trans., 1973). P. Bizzell & B. Herzberg (Editor), Rhetorical Traditions (pp. 1210–1226). Boston, Mass.: Medford / St. Martin. (Original work from 1953). Let's consider a glimpse at them one by one. Dialogue vs Monologue, the first principle of the dialogue perspective, is that communication should be dialogue, not Monologue. Lev Jakbinsky argued that when the audience actively attracted speakers through questions, even situations of public speaking often became dialogues. He even argued that non-verbal behaviour (e.g. nodding and consent) served as feedback to the speaker and even contributed to the dialogue. Yakbinsky, L.P. (1997). Interactive language. (M. Eskin, Trance). PMLA, 112 (2), 249-256. (Original work from 1923). Overall, the approach to the experience of speaking in public as a dialogue means that one is more committed as a speaker and more attention is paid to the reaction of the audience, which in turn leads to more active viewers. The meaning is in people, not in words. Part of the dialogue process in speaking publicly is recognizing that you and your audience can differ in the way you see your speech. Helmut Geisner and Edith Slembeck (1986) discussed Gessner's idea of responsibility or the idea that the meaning of words must be mutually agreed upon by interacting with people. Talk and act together—Germany, Frankfurt: screenplay. When you take the word "dog" and think of a soft, hairy pet and the animal that attacked the audience as a child, you perceive the world from a completely different perspective. As a speaker, you should write your audience-aware message and use your feedback to determine to the best of your ability, whether the intended meaning has been preserved. To successfully communicate the meaning you want, you need to know a lot about your audience and be able to choose the language that best suits the context. You cannot predict how each audience will interpret a particular word, but for example, using teen slang when speaking to an audience in a senior centre can affect your ability to convey meaning clearly. You can see that it is high.

CONTEXTS AND SOCIAL SITUATIONS

Russian scholar Mikhail Berktin points out that human interaction follows cultural norms and rules. Bakhtin, M. (2001a). Problems with the audio genre. (V. W. McGee, Trans., 1986). In P. Bizzell & B. Herzberg (ed.), Rhetorical Traditions (pp. 1227–1245). Boston, MA: Bedford / St. Martin. (Original work, published in 1953.); Bakhtin, M. (2001b). Marxism and philosophy of language. (L. Matejka& amp; I.R. Titunik, Trans., 1973). P. Bizzell & B. Herzberg (Editor), Rhetorical Traditions (pp. 1210–1226). Boston, MA: Medford / St. Martin. (Original work from 1953). How you approach people, which words we choose, and how we convey our language depends on different speaking contexts and social situations. On September 8, 2009, President Barack Obama gave a speech to school children at http://www.whitehouse.gov/mediaresources/ PreparedSchoolRemarks. If you look at the address, he gave to children nationwide and the speech at adults, you see many differences. These different speeches are needed because the audience (speaking to children and adults) has different experiences and knowledge. Ultimately, good public speaking is about taking into account the cultural background of the audience and engaging the audience from their own perspective.

CHAPTER NO. 2

EFFICIENCY

EFFICIENCY THROUGH CHANGE OF PITCH

Before we start, let's explain what the word "pitch" means. Pitch is the pitch of a voice and is very important in American English. Have you considered how to use the tone when you speak English? If not, this can be one of the main reasons why you don't sound natural yet! We use to pitch to express emotions and attitudes through changes in intonation and speech tone. Also use the pitch to express stress or to make individual syllables longer, bigger, and higher.

(If you are not yet familiar with word stress and how it works, sign up for a free 5-day email course: In 5 days it will sound more natural in English.) Here is a brief overview. Longer, more significant and higher pitch.Very important: do not forget this high pitch.Many non-native speakers change long and loud tones, but completely forget high sounds or ignore them.Why is that? Well, English has pitch variations that are different from other languages. Some languages have more pitch variations than English, and others were less.

WHY YOU NEED TO CONTROL YOUR PITCH

To sound more natural in English, you need to be able to control the pitch. The reasons are as follows. Many non-native speakers sound somewhat robotic when speaking because their voices do not have large pitch fluctuations. Their sound is rather flat and sounds a bit mechanical like a robot. We call that a monotonous voice. Not expressive, not interesting, not interesting. Native English speakers often have this flat pitch because pitch fluctuations do not make up a significant part of the mother tongue sound.

The pitch is created and used in every language for different purposes. If you are not a singer, you will probably generate the pitch subconsciously. In English, all sentences use (both female and male) pitch variations. (Listening to a man whose native language is English sounds just like me. For example, listen to videos by male comedians like Jimmy Fallon, Jimmy Kimmel and Stephen Colbert.) If you haven't created this pitch variation in your speech, those who listen to you will find it difficult to understand. Native speakers expect this pitch to change, especially with accented words and accented syllables. Apart from speaking clearly, your pitch affects your people's perception. Pitch is significant for clear communication!

EFFICIENCY THROUGH CHANGE OF PACE

Hear how he clarifies the point of religion.

WI "rock" and "pounding"! Now calm down, now upset,

He stamps "He jumps".

-Robert Burns, Holy Mass.

Latin Americans have left words that do not have an exact equivalent in our language. That's why we accepted it. The body doesn't change.

So far, its use has mainly been limited to vowel and music arts, but it is not surprising to hear that the tempo applies to more specific matters. It is because it perfectly shows the true meaning of the word that the car is moving slowly. A weapon that fires 600 times a minute fires at a fast pace. The old muzzleloader, which took three minutes to load, was spinning at a slow speed. All musicians understand this principle. Singing a half note takes longer than playing the eighth note.

Today, the pace is a significant factor for working on a good platform. Because when the speaker communicates the entire address at approximately the same speed, he steals one of the primary means of emphasis and strength. Baseball pitchers, cricket bowlers and tennis servers all know how important it is to change the pace at which a ball is delivered - the changing pace - so that standard speakers have to watch their performance.

CHANGE OF TEMPO LENDS NATURALNESS TO THE DELIVERY

As explained in the Monotony chapter, nature, or at least the nature that looks natural, is highly desirable, and continual changes in pace can make a significant contribution to establishing it. Miss Margaret Anglin's stage manager, Howard Lindsay, recently told current authors that changing the speed is one of the most effective tools for actors. While it must be admitted that the stiff mouth of many actors shows a cloudy mirror, the speaker is still good at studying the use of tempo.

However, there are more basic and useful sources for studying nature. When it is lost, it is a trait that is robbed and shy. The cause is the mutual discussion of all breeding circles. This is a standard we work on both on stage and on the platform. Of course, there are individual differences, but this will show up in a future phase. Much of the interest deviates from the general comments when speakers and actors reproduce all the variations of the conversation that are normally found in everyday life - every whisper, growl, pause, silence, explosion. The naturalness of a speech is more than a faithful reproduction of nature - it is a reproduction of a typical part of a natural work that is really representative of the whole. Realistic story writers understand this when writing dialogues. And that has to be taken into account when looking for nature by changing pace. Suppose you want to speak the first sentence of the next sentence slowly and the second sentence quickly to observe the naturalness of the effect. Then speak both at the same speed and note the differences. I can't remember what I did with a knife. Oh, now I remember giving it to Mary.

Here you can see that tempo changes often occur in the same sentence because the pace applies to individual words, phrases and groups of sentences, as well as to the main part of public speaking.

EFFICIENCY THROUGH INFLECTION

Herbert Spencer explained that "cadence" (which means the modulation of the speech tone in the language) is "a continuous commentary of emotions on the sentence of intelligence". We can see how true this is since the slight shading of the top and bottom of the voice reflects that it communicates more precisely what we mean than our words. The expressive power of language is literally multiplied by this subtle power to shade the tone of the voice, and this shade of voice we call flexion.

Pitch changes in words are even more critical because they are more subtle than pitch changes in phrases. In fact, one cannot practice without the other. Mere words are just so many broken bricks that they become paving stones, garages or cathedrals. It is the power of refraction that changes the meaning of words in old sayings: "As you say, it is not what you say."

Mrs. Jameson, a Shakespeare commentator, gave a sharp example of the impact of the transformation. First, a quick, quick questioning - "Are you failing?" Then, along with a praise note - A surprising accent in which the word "We failed" is primarily emphasized - iwi fails. Finally, she realized that I was convinced that what I was convinced was real reading - we would fail - in a single time, immediately with the problem, as she said, but the sound to a deep, deep, a determined tone that dissolves: Why it fails is all over. "

This most expressive element of our language is ultimately mastered to achieve the naturalness of speaking a foreign language, and its correct use depends on the natural and flexible expression of the mother tongue—the main element. Without a variety of bends, the sound is wooden and monotonous.

There are two types of inflexions, ascending and descending, but these two are very shaded or combined, so there are as many types as represented by one or two lines in a straight or curved line.

Sharp rising
Long rising
Level
Long falling
Sharp falling
Sharp rising and falling
Sharp falling and rising
Hesitating

These can change indefinitely and are only used to explain which combinations of these two simple audio changes can be affected. It is impossible to tabulate different inflexions that help different express shades of thoughts and emotions. Here are some suggestions along with a plethora of exercises to practice with, but the only real ways to master flexion are through observation, experimentation, and practice. For example, take the general sentence, "Oh, he's fine." Notice how rising bends can take place to express light praise, polite doubts, or disagreements. Second, it should be noted that the same words spoken infrequently changing inflexions may indicate certainty, personality approval, or enthusiastic praise. Generally speaking, flexing your voice means mistrust and uncertainty, and a critical flexion suggests that you are convinced of your position.

Students do not want their speech to be labelled "not bad". If you provoke these words long and calmly, the address is stimulated quite deeply. Say goodbye to the fictional people you think will meet again tomorrow. You will never see a dear friend again. Notice the difference in refraction. "I had a good time." When a frivolous woman speaks at the end of a formal tea, it takes an entirely different break than the same words spoken between lovers who enjoy themselves. When repeating, imitate the two characters and observe the differences.

In the following short excerpt from "Anthony, the Absolute" note how easy and quick the diffraction is.

Every night after the ship left Vancouver, and he had a round table in the middle of the smoking-room. So, he drinks coffee and liqueur and keeps all the subjects known to the human mind. Every issue is its subject. He is an older man, has a bad face, and his left eyelid is hanging. They say he's in the British Army Judges somewhere in Malaysia and drinks more than they're good for them.

Please provide the following two choices seriously and note how the changes differ from the above. Second, reread this selection slightly and note that changes in attitude are represented by changes in diffraction. If you read Plutarch's sublime facts, the selfish acts of the lines of poetry, or the thrill of heroic legends, it's no longer a fairytale land - I've seen it collapse. -Wendell Phillips. Thoughts feel deeper than all speech and more profound than all thoughts. You can never teach what you have shown from soul to soul.

CHAPTER NO. :3

THINGS TO CARE AND HAVE ATTENTION

PAUSE AND POWER

The real job of a literary artist is to knit and weave the meaning. Thus, each sentence first enters a kind of node through successive phrases and is then resolved and deleted according to the paused purpose.

-George Saintsbury, English prose style and other essays.

It has a unique value that is expressed in silence. In other words, the music of the movement continues while the voice is waiting to manage it, the same delicacy is required, which must be based on every perfect prose rhythm with its delicacy and compensation. If there is no compensation, the suspension is not provided. . . There is a feeling of trembling and lack as if the pins and fasteners had fallen off.

-John Franklin Jenung, working principles of rhetoric.

A language break is not just silence but eloquent silence. When the man says, "It's a deep pleasure. It was allowed to speak to you tonight and, um, I should say" - it's not paused; it stumbles. It is possible that the speaker is working, but that is not the cause. On the other hand, one of the most important ways to improve public speaking is to take a break before and after or before and after important words and phrases. Nobody can be a convincing speaker and ignore this principle. One of the most important things that were guessed from hearing the great speaker. Examine this potential device until you absorb and assimilate it.

This rhetorical pause principle seems easy to understand and apply, but due to the long experience of training college men and mature speakers when the device was first described, it has proven to be more difficult for the average person to understand than when it is spoken in Hindustani. Maybe because we are not looking to devour the fruits of experience if we impressively stand on a plate of authority. We like to pick fruit for ourselves -

it not only tastes good; we never forget this tree! Fortunately, this is not a difficult task. In this example, trees grow around us.

One pleads for another's cause: "This person, my friend, has made this wonderful sacrifice for you and me." Surprisingly, the pause is not the strength of this statement. See how he gathered the reluctance and impression to convey the word "for you and me". Repeat this sentence without a break. Lost effectiveness? Not surprisingly, during this planned break, the speaker focuses on the ideas he is trying to express. He doesn't dare to ponder his thoughts for a moment. Rather, its attraction, its opulence and its divinity concentrate its thoughts and feelings considerably on the victims who are forced by its charm. Concentration is a big word here - without it, a break cannot be fully marked. Stopping efficiently achieves one or all of the following four results:

THE PAUSE ALLOWS THE SPEAKER TO GATHER THEIR STRENGTH BEFORE DELIVERING THE FINAL VOLUME

It is often dangerous to enter the fight without stopping or waiting for recruits. Take the Custer massacre as an example. The match can be illuminated by holding the match under the lens and focusing the sun's rays. If you move the lens back and forth quickly, don't expect the game to burn. The lens collects heat during a break. Your thoughts won't ignite your listeners unless you take a break to concentrate for a moment or twice. Maple trees and gas wells are rarely constantly tapped. If a more substantial river is required, a pause is made, of course, there is time to collect reserves, and the tree or well is opened again, resulting in a more substantial river.

Use the same common sense in your head. If you want your thoughts to be particularly effective, take a short break before saying something, concentrate your mental energy, and then express yourself with new vitality. Carlyle was right. "Do not speak. I implore you passionately until your thoughts ripen softly. Silence builds up your strength. Language is silver, and silence is gold, language is human, silence is divine."

Silence is the father of language. That should be. Many of our public speeches have no father. They graze without breaks or breaks. Like the tennis stream, they run forever. Listen to the conversations of the young children, the corner policeman and the family at the table and pay attention to the effects. So, look at the number of poses they use naturally. When we stand in front of the audience, we throw most of the natural forms of expression into the wind and work on artificial effects. Return to the natural path and take a break.

PAUSE PREPARES THE JUDGE'S MIND TO RECEIVE YOUR MESSAGE

Herbert Spencer said that the entire universe is in motion. So, it is - and all perfect motion is rhythm. Part of rhythm is rest. Rest follows activity all through nature. Instances: day and night; spring - summer - autumn - winter; a period of rest between breaths; an instant of complete rest between heart beats. Pause, and give the attention-powers of your audience a rest. What you say after such a silence will then have a great deal more effect.

When your country cousins come to town, the noise of a passing car will awaken them, though it seldom affects a seasoned city dweller. By the continual passing of cars his attention-power has become deadened. In one who visits the city but seldom, attention-value is insistent. To him the noise comes after a long pause; hence its power. To you, dweller in the city, there is no pause; hence the low attention-value. After riding on a train several hours, you will become so accustomed to its roar that it will lose its attention-value, unless the train should stop for a while and start again. If you attempt to listen to a clock-tick that is so far away that you can barely hear it, you will find that at times you are unable to distinguish it, but in a few moments the sound becomes distinct again. Your mind will pause for rest whether you desire it to do so or not.

FORCE

"However, it is appropriate to be careful. There is no indifference, no certification, no pain, and the rash enthusiasm in a good society was nothing less than moral injustice.

-Byron and Don Juan.

You participated in a fair play, but they didn't move or grab you. They couldn't "get over" about the theater. In short, their message did not come across the traces of the audience. They had no blows or bumps - they had no strength. Of course, all of this triggers a big-letter disaster on every platform, not just on-stage production. All of these presentations only exist for the audience and if they don't guess - and the expression is good - it's no excuse to live. Don't live long either.

WHAT IS FORCE?

Some of our most obvious words reveal the secret meaning that is being investigated, and this is one of them. First of all, we have to recognize the difference between internal and external forces. One is the cause and the other is the result. One is spiritual and the other is physical. In this important respect, the power of living things is different from the power of inanimate things. Human power is expressed from the inside out and is a different type of power than Shimose powder that does not explode and is waiting for an effect. Despite the sensitivity to external stimuli, the true source of human strength lies in itself. This may seem like "only psychology", but has a very practical connection to public speaking.

Not only can we distinguish the difference between human power and mere physical power, but their true nature should not be confused with what may or may not accompany them. For example, volume is not a performance, but performance can be accompanied by noise. The Me sound never made a good speech, but there are moments when great audio power can be used with enormous effects - not moments, but mind you. There is no violent athletic strength - but strength can lead to violent movement. Hamlet advised the players:

Also, don't look up in the air with your hands. But use everything carefully. Because in very strong currents, storms and (as I could say) a whirlwind of your passion, you have to gain and produce a temper that could make it smooth. Oh, that offends me on the soul. I hear a lumpy wig buddy that tears apart the passion of tearing the ears of the base ring, torn up, very ragged. In most cases, it can only show ridiculous shows and sounds. I would have had such a guy flogged for a termant. You are more enthusiastic than Herod. Please avoid.

Don't domesticate too much; leave your discretion to your tutor. Match action for words, words for actions. With this special observance, you are not the humility of nature. It is too much for the purpose of playing with a "mirror of nature" both at the beginning and now at the end, which shows the own qualities of virtue and brightens itself. And the body of that time, its shape and its pressure. Well, that can be over the top or slow, but it makes a wicked laugh, but it can't make wise sadness. The accusation that your allowances must make the entire theatre of others difficult. Oh, I saw some people playing - and others praised and very disturbed - no Christian accents, no Christian, pagan or human walks. Some of the nature travelers didn't make people too worried but shouted that I thought they didn't. They mimicked humanity very badly.

One sits in a hole or parquet.

Power is cause and effect. The inner force that must precede the outer force is a combination of four elements that work gradually. Power comes primarily from conviction. It would help if you were convinced of the truth or importance or importance of what you want to say before forcing the offer. It has to stick to your beliefs before you can catch your audience. I am convinced of the trust.

Many of the successes of the public platforms on Saturday night after Winston Spencer Churchill-Churchill and Roosevelt in an article on "England's TR" are due to its widespread use. Whatever is at hand, these men will initially make you believe that you are the most important on the planet. So, they say to the audience, "Don't do that."Such a story win. And it is his energetic, wild, offensive attitude that distinguishes and supports our great career as a leading platform.But let's take a closer look at the origin of the inner force. How does a belief affect those who feel it?

1 Hamlet, Act III, scene 2.

It is these string tensions, muscle knots and contractions before spring that give the audience a feeling for the restraint of the speaker. On some really great points, the speakers don't say this, revealing the internal dynamo. When loosening something can result from such accumulated forces. And it alarms the audience hanging on the speaker's lips after the next word. After all, it's all a question of masculinity, as stuffed animals have no certainty or emotional tension. If it is covered with sawdust, move away from the platform.

From this tension of conviction grows the determination to get the audience to share this tension. The purpose is the backbone of power. Without it, the sound is sloppy - it may shimmer, but it is the dazzling colour of a jellyfish without spikes. When you hold your audience, you have to hold on to your determination.

FEELING AND ENTHUSIASM

Enthusiasm is a harmony with the secrets that remain in the production of genius.

-Isaac Disraeli, literary character.

Of course, when you talk to a group of scientists about a topic like a butterfly wing or a street structure, your problem won't cause too much emotion for you or your audience. These are purely spiritual issues. But if you want men to vote on child labor abolition measures, or if you're going to encourage them to take up arms for free, you have to meet them directly. We lie on a soft bed, sit near a radiator on a cold day, eat cherry pie and take care of one of the other sexes. Not because you conclude that it is right, but because you feel that it is correct. Nobody except indigestion will choose a meal from the table. Our feelings determine what we eat and how we behave in general. Humans are animals that express opinions. Therefore, a speaker's ability to get a man to act depends almost entirely on his ability to touch emotions.

Black mothers who auction off how children are sold from slave to slave have erased some of America's most inspiring speeches. The mother had no knowledge of language technology, but she had something better than all techniques, more effective than reason, emotions. Big statements around the world are not made with tariff cuts or postal budgets. A living language is full of emotional power. Prosperity and peace are eloquent and poor developers. It's an exciting place to talk when big mistakes are corrected when people's hearts burn with passion. Patrick Henry made an immortal speech. Because they were looking for freedom in a pioneering crisis, he was honest and passionate enough to shout, "Give me freedom, give me death." If he had been alive today and called a judge back, his fame would have been different.

THE POWER OF ENTHUSIASM

Political parties hire bands and pay applause for it - they claim that it is more effective to arouse enthusiasm for voices than to infer from it. I know how good it depends on the audience, but there is no doubt about the infectiousness of enthusiasm. New York watchmakers have tried two watch advertising series. Others spoke in favour of the excellent construction, quality, durability and guarantee of a watch. The other went to a "proud watch" and held on to the owner's joy and pride. The recent series saw double the sales of the former. A locomotive salesman told the writer that the emotional appeal of selling railroad engines was stronger than discussions based on mechanical excellence.

The grace taught at school, expensive ornaments, the study of language, the mechanisms of shock and disgust, your own life and your wives, children and the fate of the country depend on the decisions made at the time, And even the word genius feels itself condemned and reluctant, like the existence of higher qualities: logic, high intention, firm determination, courageous spirit, speaking with the tongue, light from the eyes and conveys all traits and urges the whole person for the entire topic - that is eloquent, or rather, it is greater and more significant than any eloquence: it is action, noble, sublime, like God's action.

Some time ago in the northwest, one of the current writers strolled through the village streets after dinner and noticed that the crowd in the corner of a glove box heard "wrong" conversations. Observers remembered Emerson's advice to learn from everyone we met and stopped listening to the attraction of this speaker. He sold hair tonics that he allegedly found in Arizona. He took off his hat, showed what this remedy did for him, washed his face, was as harmless as water, and enthusiastically added half a dollar of a silver surge to the benefits. When he offered the crowd a hair tonic, he asked why men were outnumbered by women. Nobody knew. He explained that women wore thinner soles and made good electrical connections to Mother Earth, and men wore thick, dry feet that did not transmit the electricity of the earth to the body. Male hair did not have the correct amount of electrical food but died and fell. Of course, he had an agent - a small copper plate that had to be nailed to the bottom of the shoe. He was enthusiastic and crisp and described how desirable it was to avoid hair loss and pay homage to the copper plate. It may seem strange that the story is cold printed, but the speaker's enthusiasm wiped out the audience with him, worried that they were the owners of these magical records. They were crushed around the booth!

Emerson's proposal was well received - observers again saw the great persuasiveness of the enthusiasm!

The enthusiasm sent millions of crusaders to the holy land and repurchased it from the Saracens. Interest has forced Europe to wage a 30-year war against religion. The excitement sent three small boats that sailed the unknown world to the shores of the New World. When Napoleon's army was exhausted and prevented from climbing into the Alps, the Little Corps chief stopped them and ordered the band to play Marseille. There were no Alps under nervous tension.

CONCENTRATION IN DELIVERY

Attention is the mental eye microscope. The performance can be high or low. The field of vision is narrow or wide. When high power is used, attention is limited within very limited limits, but its operation is very intense and absorbent. There is little to see, but some of them, whether perceptible or thoughtful, are focused and observed by "burning out" mental energy and activity. The object was illuminated, warmed and illuminated. The impression is so deep that it can never be erased. This kind of attention is an important condition for the most productive mental work.

-Daniel Putnam, psychology.

Tap lightly on your chest and rub your head back and forth. If coordination is not well developed, it will be confusing, if not impossible. The brain needs specialised training before it can efficiently do more than one thing at a time. Although it appears that the hair is split between the north and northwest corners, some psychologists argue that the brain cannot think of two different thoughts at precisely the same time. What seems to be at the same time is a high-speed rotation from the first thought to the second and back again. You have to go from one hand to the other.

Regardless of the psychological truth of this controversy, there is no denying that the moment the attention is clearly projected before the second or third idea, the mind loses measurable influence on an idea.

A disadvantage, which is just as harmful as a normal speaker, is trying to think about the next sentence when speaking, which reduces the concentration. As a result, they start the sentence strong and end weakly. In a well-prepared speech, the emphasis is usually at the end of the sentence. However, important words require an important phrase that you will not get if you show your focus by jumping too early on what is being said next. Concentrate all mental energy on the current sentence. Remember that if you distract attention from what you say, from what you say, your audience will also withdraw because the heart of your audience follows your heart very carefully. You may not be doing this consciously and deliberately, but you certainly won't be focusing on the little things themselves. It is fatal if actors or speakers cross the bridge too early.

Of course, this doesn't mean that you shouldn't take a quick look ahead with a natural pause in your speech - they're as important as looking forward while driving. Warnings are a completely different kind. Do not consider the following sentence while speaking a sentence. Get it from the right source. The broadside cannot be sent without concentration - this is the cause of the explosion. Preparation stores and focuses on thoughts and emotions. Breaks during the transfer quickly accumulate proactively for active attacks. Do not speak at the moment of the actual speech. Share your attention and strength.

This question of the effect of the inner person on the outer person needs further words, especially as a touching focus.

"What are you reading, sir?" Answered Hamlet. "Words. Words. Words." It is an old problem worldwide. A call for a mechanical word is not an expression of the stretch. Have you ever noticed that a remembered speech is usually free? You have heard inefficient actors, lawyers, preachers and mechanical rhythms. Their problem is spiritual - they just sound mechanical and not intense, which gives them honesty and conviction. A painful experience for the audience and the speakers! Parrots are also eloquent. Let us teach Shakespeare again in the dishonest prayer of King Hamlet's uncle. He points out:

My words jump up, and my thoughts stay down.

The truth is that your words as speakers need to be reborn every time they are spoken. Dr Russell Conwell's lecture "Like a

Diamond Tomorrow" 5000 times. Such a speech is not only the need to say something but from the full patent reason that it arises from concentrated thinking and emotions. Don't lose anything. If the thought under your word is warm, fresh, spontaneous, and part of you, your remark has breath and life. It is only a result. Do not try to get results without stimulating the cause.

Are you asking how to focus? Think of the words themselves and concentric linguistic siblings. Think about how a lens collects and radiates concentrically within a particular circle. It focuses them through the payout process. It may sound like a harsh phrase, but the unfocused man has never learned what his will is, is a nervous wreck or what his willpower is for.

You need to concentrate by resolutely diverting your attention from everything else. If you focus your thoughts on the pain, you may be suffering from, and the pain will become more intense. "Count your blessings," they increase. The tennis game will gradually improve as you focus on shots. Concentrating means being aware of only one thing and doing nothing else. If you notice that you cannot do this, something is wrong - be mindful of this first. After eliminating the cause, the symptoms disappear. Read the chapter "Willpower". Grow your will through joy and action. Concentrate - and you win.

CHAPTER 4:

AUDIENCE ANALYSIS

WHAT IS AN AUDIENCE ANALYSIS?

One of the consequences of the First Amendment, which protects our free say, is that we focus on what we mean. Is the audience interested in your idea as a speaker? Can you see how your speech applies to your life and interests? Speaking in public is an everyday activity in which the speaker and the audience interact. In order for your expression to be heard relatively, you need to build a relationship with your audience. Scholars Sprague, Stuart and Border explain: "Speakers don't speak to the audience; they create meaning with the audience." Sprague, J., Stuart, D. and Bodary, D. (2010). Speaker's Handbook, 9th edition. Boston, Mass.: Wadsworth Cengage, the success of a speech, depends on how the audience receives and understands it.

Consider listening to a speech that sounds "canned" or a speech that has been flattened because the audience "didn't understand". This can happen because the speaker did not view public speaking as a general activity. To make matters worse, a lack of audience attention can be confused by marginalized listeners by making jokes or offensive words that listeners don't like. The best way to reduce the risk of this situation is to do a crowd analysis while preparing your speech.

The target group analysis collects information about your target group so that you can understand their needs, expectations, beliefs, values, attitudes and reasonable opinions. In this chapter, we will first examine some of the reasons why audience analysis is essential. The following sections describe the three types of audience analysis and some of the techniques for performing audience analysis. Finally, it is examined how you can use the target group analysis not only during language creation but also during the transmission.

THREE TYPES OF AUDIENCE ANALYSIS

Target audience analysis does not guarantee misjudgment, but it can help you choose the right topic, language, presentation style, and other aspects of your speech. The more you know about your audience, the more they can meet their interests and needs. While learning by gathering information is undoubtedly limited and must be recognized before making assumptions, knowing how to collect and use information through audience analysis is an essential skill for a successful speaker.

DEMOGRAPHIC ANALYSIS

As mentioned earlier, demographic information includes factors such as gender, age group, marital status, race and ethnicity, and socioeconomic status. In public lectures, you will probably know how many students are male and female, how old they are, and so on. But how can you evaluate the demographics of an audience in advance if there is no previous contact with the audience? You can often ask the person or organization that invited you to speak. They can tell you a lot about the demographics of the people who are expected to hear your story.

Regardless of which method you use to collect demographic data, you pay homage right from the start. For example, if you collect information about whether your audience has been divorced, keep in mind that not everyone wants to answer your question. You cannot ask them for it. You also cannot assume that you do not like to discuss topics. Data protection must be allowed.

CHAPTER NO. :5

IMPORTANT THINGS ABOUT SELECTION

DISTINCTNESS AND PRECISION OF UTTERANCE

The man speaks to God.

-Hesiod, words and days.

And the language modes are endless and expand the word field from side to side.

-Homer, Iliad.

In common parlance, the terms "pronunciation", "pronunciation" and "articulation" are synonymous, but since actual pronunciation involves three different processes, syllables or groups of syllables that refer to articulation can be defined as utterances—accent, pronunciation.Clear and accurate language is one of the most important considerations about public language. How ridiculous it is to hear a speaker shouting "indistinct seriousness" under the controversial delusion of speaking to the audience! Tell me? Communicating means communicating, and how can you actually communicate without distinguishing every word?A smooth pronunciation results either from physical deformities or from habits. The surgeon or the surgeon's dentist can correct the malformation, but your own will to work with a drill through introspection and resolution breaks the pattern. Everything depends on whether it's worth it.Speech errors are so extensive that freedom is an exception. It is painful to hear how speakers separate the King's English. As Kallang once said, they often knock me out if they don't really kill it.

A Canadian employee wrote in a homiletical review: "While at school, an English classmate gave a country church on Sunday. A mission rally took place next Monday. When I gave" Hoods and Hand ", I thought I was doing my duty to the mission "But the Lord needed more. At the end of the meeting, a young woman told her friend seriously. If you give the mission pigs and chickens, that's more than most people can afford." "

Appearing in front of an audience that is still happy to pass the time from home and heaven is unbearable for every man, and in other words, Waldo Messaros does not rest in hell. Those who do not show enough self-knowledge to see such a glow for themselves are not doing it wrong, and there is not enough self-control to fix it, and no business to teach others. If he can't do better, he should be silent. If he doesn't feel better, he should be silent.

Apart from incurable physical mistakes - and nowadays only a few people are incurable - every problem is a will. The catalogue of those who have achieved the impossible with faithful work is as touching as the reputation of a warrior. "The less you are, the more you have to get out of your presence," says Nathan Shepherd.

ARTICULATION

Articulation is the formation and combination of the basic sounds of speech. While the three millionth word that makes up the English vocabulary sounds clear, it sounds like a terrible task, but getting started is very easy. Learn to speak correctly and quickly switch from one to the other, each of the 44 underlying tones of our language.

There are four reasons why so many speakers find it painful to articulate—ignorance of elemental tones. Sounds can hardly be distinguished in the same way—sloppy, lazy use of vocal organs and uncanny will. Anyone who is still their own master will know how to treat each of these shortcomings. Vowels are the source of the most annoying mistakes, especially when diphthongs are found. Who hasn't heard of the mistakes Oliver Wendell Holmes makes in this unique poem?

Learn careless lips to talk about the soap that is accused of going beyond the desired area. Your e-decree will be excluded from your beautiful apartment. Steer his boat, think it is a boat he is not so strict about, and call his coat. She forgave one of the prides of our classic city. Who said most of Cambridge instead?

But knitted her forehead and stamped her angry foot. To hear what the teacher calls the root the root.

The previous examples are all monosyllabic, but what we don't understand is the result of the combination of sounds that don't belong together. For example, no one finds it difficult to say beauty, but many continue to express their commitments as if it were either a duty or a duty. Not only by untrained speakers but also by column collimations and cute and clean, even great speakers, it can be as embarrassing as a less conspicuous person.

Such things are almost unintentional mistakes, not pure ignorance. The ears don't listen to the lips. For a foreigner, you must note that the elementary sound does not indicate the pronunciation of branch, cough, roughness. Although it is a complex English pronunciation, there is no excuse for the gentle utterances of simple vowels that shape the life and beauty of our language at the same time. People who have difficulty speaking clearly should hold their tongues.

Consonants can only cause serious problems for those who do not closely observe the spelling of the word. Nobody can say Jacopo, Baptiste, Seven, Aluus or other satisfaction as negligence.

"Whoever has greed makes greed" is an Anglophobic priest's account of a familiar scripture. After pronouncing the name of Humphrey Davy in, the French wanted to write a letter to a prominent Englishman who addressed the letter "Seram Fridavi".

ACCENTUATION

The accent is the emphasis on the corresponding syllable of a word. This is commonly referred to as pronunciation. For example, if a word is accented with "-vote" instead of "invite", the word is correctly misspelled but is actually a form of pronunciation, namely violation.

Learning large vocabulary and responding to changes in usage is a one-time task. But watchful ears, etymological studies and dictionary habits prove to be powerful helpers for tasks that cannot be completed in the end.

ENUNCIATION

The correct pronunciation is the complete utterance of all sounds of a syllable or a word. Wrong articulations, such as dew pigeons, give the vowels of words and syllables the crazy sound. Or combine the two sounds incorrectly. An incorrect pronunciation is an incomplete utterance of a syllable or word, and the sound that is left out or added is usually a consonant. To say necessity instead of necessity is a misnomer. What you are doing is incorrect pronunciation. One is clearly articulated - that is, two sounds that should not be connected. So, give this word a positively wrong sound. The other cannot touch every note in the word, and the word sounds wrong in this way.

"My Tex" may have "splashed" in the fifth and sixth verses of Chapter 2 of Titus II, and the subject of my discussion is "The Government of Al Holmes". ""

What did this preacher do with the last consonant? This indiscriminate filing of essential sounds is just as uncomfortable as the usual practice of putting words together so that they lose their personality and clarity. Darker, lighter, face down, doncher don't have to make any comments, especially since they are familiar with laminating.

METHODS OF DELIVERY

The crown of discourse, the end is its delivery. All preparations are visible in this direction, but the audience is waiting for what the speaker will be judged by the whole force of the speaker's life converges on his or her speaker. The logical sharpness of the compilation of facts on the subject, the rhetorical institutions that order language, the control that is achieved through the use of the body as the only means of expression, the wealth of acquisition and experience - all of these are events. The fact is that he sends his message home to the listener. ... delivery time is "the best, inevitable time" for a speaker. It is this fact that makes the lack of adequate preparation so negligent. And this sends an immaterial thrill through the entire presence of the speaker if he succeeds - it forgets her suffering for the joy that her mother gives birth to her son

There are four basic ways to distribute addresses. All others are one or more of these modifications: reading from manuscripts, committing written language, language from memory, writing from notes and instant communication. It is impossible to say which form of distribution is best for all speakers in all situations - decide for yourself, take into account the opportunity, the type of audience, the type of topic, the time and subject restrictions. It must be, however, warn you not to forgive the self-declaration too much. Boldly say to yourself: I can try what others can do. The daring spirit conquers where others fall, and challenging work challenges happiness.

READING FROM MANUSCRIPT

This method deserves the brief simplicity of a book on public speaking. However, there are so many people who take this broken trail of support that we have to talk about "reading language" here.

SPEAKING FROM NOTES

The third and most common shipping method is probably the best for beginners as well. Talking about the note is not an ideal delivery, but learn to swim in the shallow water before going outside on the ropes.

Make a clear plan for the discourse and setpoints as a short lawyer assignment or summary of preachers. Here is a straightforward example note:

SUBJECT AND PREPARATION

You wrote a speech. Congratulation! Let us now consider how you can present the speech and prepare it accordingly. First, decide how you want the speech to be presented. Read the newly created language literally from the script? Or do you remember that? Or do you easily read outlines and notes?In the first speech, it helps to be fully typed and ready to read literally in front of the crowd. You can be safer by putting the exact wording right in front of you.

Literal reading from scripts has its drawbacks. Eye contact with the viewer can be limited. This allows your audience to separate from your words and your speaker more quickly. In addition, the language that is read directly from scripts and manuscripts often feels stubborn or stiff.

MEMORIZING YOUR SPEECH

You can remember language as well as dialogues or monologues in one piece. Getting rid of reading one or more sheets of paper loses some of the stiffness associated with understanding the speech from a script. It is less likely to fit in your hands, giving you more freedom to position your body when you deliver a speech and is more engaging.

However, one of the most significant drawbacks to remembering language is the unexpected stage horror, which can be utterly addictive without remembering the vocabulary. It is never painful to have a copy of your speech on hand when you want to remember it.

SPEAKING EXTEMPORANEOUSLY FROM NOTES

The intermediate point between reading from a script and remembering language is reading from a note. By preparing the outline with key points or the order in which some note cards are presented, you can use the safety net to open your body freely. When speaking of a note, you may need to hold hands to hold the record and keep a close eye on the viewer. Compromises are valuable because they can adopt a winning attitude that is tied to the language outline.

DEALING WITH NERVES

It is perfectly normal to be nervous when giving your first speech to a broad audience. Even the leaders of the world put butterflies in their bellies before entering the world stage. Remember to fight fear. Flushing the speech is unlikely to kill you.

Frequent practice over time can also relieve anxiety. Read the speeches to develop the memory of the muscles around phrases and sentences. You can even read your statement in front of trusted friends and colleagues. When practicing in front of a small group, you don't have to give a presentation in front of a large group. When you make your friends a test, you also have the opportunity to provide valuable feedback on what you are doing well and what needs to be improved. If you don't know what you're talking about, practice in front of a mirror. Even better, record yourself and play this recording yourself several times. Watching yourself speak is another excellent way to calm your nerves, release tension, and discover subtle facial movements and body language that could actually hurt your style.

CHAPTER NO: 6

THINGS TO REMEMBER

GROWING A VOCABULARY

Speaking in public can be a terrible experience itself, but if you feel that your vocabulary is awful, it can get worse. Increasing vocabulary can be better than speaking or writing language in public. It also helps to improve written and oral communication skills and expresses itself. If you want to improve your vocabulary for public speaking, write it down and focus on continually learning new words.

Commit regularly. If you want to improve your vocabulary, for example, due to public speaking, take a daily or weekly break. Plan a "book vocabulary" as you book the time of day to learn and use new words. I read. Although reading has been shown to expand your vocabulary, you rarely have more time to read. Plan a regular schedule, e.g. B. during lunch or before bed and make reading a habit. Underline new words.

Keep vocabulary notes. You may remember them from elementary school, but they can also help your adult life. Take notes in your notebook as you learn new words. Include definitions, parts of speech, uses, synonyms and antonyms. Write a separate sentence with each word in the vocabulary.

Learn the most common words related to public speaking. As you improve your general vocabulary, it's probably a good idea to familiarize yourself with the terms that describe public speaking itself—familiarity with terms such as props, visuals, brainstorming and immediate non-verbal communication.

Watch speaker videos or read famous speeches and write down your vocabulary. If you really want to improve your public vocabulary, learn from the best. Watch videos of lectures and presentations online and read famous statements from history. Write your favourite words and new words in a vocabulary note and consider how you can use them in your next public speech.

Use a thesaurus after writing a speech or presentation. The same vocabulary is often reused, particularly in a professional context. After creating the main text, sit in the thesaurus and search for new terms for the words you already know. Write synonyms in the vocabulary notes and make some changes by replacing some words in the text with synonyms.

MAKING CONVERSATION EFFECTIVE

W. E. Gladstone's father viewed the conversation as art and achievement. At the dining table in his house, topics of local or national interest or questions discussed were always discussed. In this way, there was a friendly confrontation of superiority in the conversation between families, and incidents observed on the street, ideas gathered from books and conclusions from personal experiences were carefully documented as material for family interaction. His first elegant conversation practice prepared young Gladstone for a career as a leader and speaker. Since our conversation is often heard by many people, the ability to speak effectively has the feeling of speaking in an efficient public.

In fact, conversations overall are probably more potent than the combined media and platforms. Socrates did not teach his great truth on the public podium but in personal conversations. Men made pilgrimages to Goethe's library and Coleridge's house and were intrigued and guided by their speech. And the cultures of many nations have been immeasurably influenced by ideas that come from their rich sources.

Most of the speech that moves the world takes place in the conversation. Diplomatic meetings, business discussions, board decisions, and corporate policy considerations affect the world's political, commercial, and economic maps, although they are usually informal discussions. It is the result of careful opinions. The severity of such a crisis is the one who first thought carefully about the words of the opponent and the protagonist.

Regardless of how important it is to gain self-control in light social conversations or for a family table, it is essential to fully recover from important meetings. Later, the information we gave on calmness, vigilance, verbal accuracy, clear meaningfulness and speaking power in relation to public speaking apply equally to conversations. A form of nervous selfishness - both are - are often competitions. An abrupt end when you have to speak a keyword is a sign of defeat. If you are confusing this trend, be sure to listen to Holmes' advice. And if you stick to the conversation, you shouldn't be dealing with these terrible worries.

Your will is carried out here because your problem is wandering attention. You need to keep your mind on the chosen conversation and categorically reject distractions from unexpected topics and events. The mistake here is a total loss of effectiveness. Concentration is the key to attractiveness and efficiency. Tally land paraphrases the rustic expression habit of using bird shots when bullets are needed - especially in times of crisis when the language is no longer available - all types of diplomacy depend on the correct application of the right words.

Looking at word derivations can often shed new light on old issues. Conversation originally meant changing the idea, but most people seem to see it as a monologue. Bronson Alcott said that many could disprove it, but there was little opposition. The first thing to remember in a conversation is that listening - respect, sympathy, and careful listening - applies to both other speakers and us. Many answers lose their meaning because the speaker is very interested in what he says.

Self-expression is refreshing. It describes the eternal impulse to decorate a totem pole, to paint, to write poems and to explain the philosophy. One of the chief joys of the conversation is the opportunity for self-expression. A good interlocutor who monopolizes all conversations is bored to deny others the pleasure of self-expression. You are praised for who is happy: you please those who listen well. The first step to improving confusion, unwieldy attitudes, ambiguity in thinking and inaccuracy in the language is to recognize your mistakes. Nobody - at least yourself - can help you if you are not aware of it.

www.ingramcontent.com/pod-product-compliance
Lightning Source LLC
Chambersburg PA
CBHW070335120526
44590CB00017B/2891